Joke & Riddle Ballyhoo

Jacqueline Horsfall

Illustrated by
Jackie Snider

Sterling Publishing Co., Inc.
New York

For Taylor

Library of Congress Cataloging-in-Publication Data Available

10 9 8 7 6 5 4 3

Published by Sterling Publishing Co., Inc.
387 Park Avenue South, New York, NY 10016
Text copyright © 2005 by Jacqueline Horsfall
Illustrations copyright © 2005 by Jackie Snider
Distributed in Canada by Sterling Publishing
C/o Canadian Manda Group, 165 Dufferin Street
Toronto, Ontario, Canada M6K 3H6
Distributed in Great Britain and Europe by Chris Lloyd at Orca Book
Services, Stanley House, Fleets Lane, Poole BH15 3AJ, England
Distributed in Australia by Capricorn Link (Australia) Pty. Ltd.
P.O. Box 704, Windsor, NSW 2756, Australia

Manufactured in the United States of America
All rights reserved

Sterling ISBN 1-4027-2547-7

For information about custom editions, special sales, premium
and corporate purchases, please contact Sterling Special Sales
Department at 800-805-5489 or specialsales@sterlingpub.com.

Contents

Beastie Bloopers

What do you call a lazy kangaroo?
  A pouch potato.

What do you call an elephant that jumps into your pool?
  The Big Dipper.

What do you feed a giant panda that's skinned its knee?
  Bamboo-boo.

What should you give a snake before putting it to bed?

A good-night hiss.

What animal should you never play cards with?

A cheetah.

What does a cheetah get when it hits its head?

A CAT scan.

What kind of jewelry do pigs wear on their legs?

Oinkle bracelets.

What's a cat's favorite pitch?
The hairball.

Why do moths make good actors?
They're attracted to the spotlight.

Where do butterflies go to dance?
The mothball.

What does a baby whale pour into its bathtub?
Blubbles.

What did the rubber duckie say to the baby whale?
"Hi, squirt!"

What do llamas wear to bed?
Pajjamas.

What do frogs wear on the way to their water beds?
Bedroom flippers.

What do you get when your pet goldfish jumps out of its bowl?
Sushi.

What do bunnies read before going to bed?
Cottontales.

What time do chickens wake up in the morning?
Five o'cluck.

Why do roosters seem so vain?
They carry their combs wherever they go.

If roosters have combs on their heads, what do rabbits have?
Harebrushes.

What did the rooster crow after a pasta dinner?
"Cock-a-noodle-doo!"

How do you get ticks off your dog?
Take away its watch.

What do sea creatures eat on their birthdays?
Crab cakes.

What do cats eat on their birthdays?
Mice-cream cones.

What happens when your cat scratches its fur off?
It's a major catastroflea.

What do you call a cat that drinks bad milk?
Sourpuss.

How do you videotape a beach party?
With a clamcorder.

What do crabs say when they're introduced at beach parties?
"Shell we dance?"

How do sharks introduce themselves at beach parties?
"Pleased to eat you."

How does Zorro protect himself from sharks?
With a swordfish.

What lives in a shell and sleeps all day?
A napping turtle.

What does a cow use for shaving?
A blade of grass.

How is the letter A like a rosebush?
They both have bees coming after them.

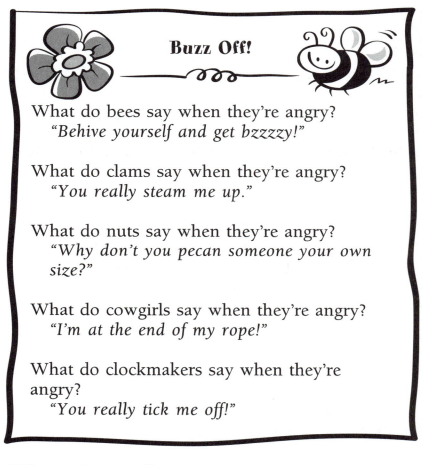

Buzz Off!

What do bees say when they're angry?
"Behive yourself and get bzzzzy!"

What do clams say when they're angry?
"You really steam me up."

What do nuts say when they're angry?
"Why don't you pecan someone your own size?"

What do cowgirls say when they're angry?
"I'm at the end of my rope!"

What do clockmakers say when they're angry?
"You really tick me off!"

Why can't you tell pigs your secrets?
They squeal.

How do hogs haul their garbage?
In pig-up trucks.

What do you call a pig in the middle of the highway?
A road hog.

How do grizzlies ride their horses?
Bearback.

What should you do if a bear cuts himself?
Call his paw.

Where do you find frogs at football games?
On the cheerleaping squads.

When are chickens penalized at basketball games?
When they cross the fowl line.

How did the kangaroo score at basketball?
With a jump shot.

How do dinosaurs like their prey?
Terrifried!

How do moles eat their dinners?
They dig right in.

What's the best way to keep a skunk from smelling?
Plug its nose.

What marks a turkey's burial site?
A gravystone.

Why do camels never get hungry crossing the desert?
Because of all the sand which is there.

Why do flamingos stand on one leg?
If they stood on no legs, they'd fall down!

What helps Santa fly safely through hurricanes?
His rain deer.

Fiddle-de-Riddles

What do you call a lollipop dropped on the beach?
Sandy candy.

What do you call whale soap?
Blubber scrubber.

What do you call a humpback at half price?
A whale sale.

What do you call a dog left out in the rain?
A wet pet.

What do you call a little dog that
scribbles?
A doodle poodle.

What do you call ballet leotards?
Dance pants.

What do you call a rabbit's coins?
Bunny money.

What do you call a bird that thinks it's a rabbit?
A carrot parrot.

What do you call a rodent that lives in your
bedroom?
A house mouse.

What do you call an insane flower?
A crazy daisy.

What do you call a baby sheep's jelly?
Lamb's jam.

What do you call a college for ghosts?
A ghoul school.

Yum-Yum!

What do you call a happy fruit?
A merry cherry.

What do you call skinny limas?
Lean beans.

What do you call Cheddar on a tissue?
Sneeze cheese.

What do you call a fruit drink for deer?
Moose juice.

What do you call jam on your tummy?
Belly jelly.

What do you call a tofu birthday dessert?
Fake cake.

What do you call a school course for fish?
Bass class.

What do you call an elf that milks cows?
A dairy fairy.

What do you call food at a dairy farm?
Cow chow.

What do you call green whiskers?
A weird beard.

What do you call a messy corn eater?
A cob slob.

What do you call an insect's coffee cup?
A bug mug.

What do you call a flock of seagulls?
A bird herd.

What do you call a soup made of butterflies?
Moth broth.

What do you call shellfish gossip?
Crab blab.

What do you call a song played at night?
A moon tune.

What do you call stardust?
Twinkle sprinkle.

What do you call a geyser?
A mountain fountain.

What do you call a wheelbarrow full of stones?
A boulder holder.

What do you call a plump chimpanzee?
A chunky monkey.

What do you call a wet bear?
A drizzly grizzly.

What do you call a bandit that
leaves a slimy trail?
A slug thug.

Sports Shorts

What do you call a tarantula on ice skates?
A spider glider.

What do you call the rubber disk in a waterfowl's
hockey game?
A duck puck.

What do you call a sailing reptile?
An alligator navigator.

What do you call an insect manager?
A roach coach.

What do you call an Olympic swim star?
A damp champ.

What do you call a cruel ruler?
  A mean queen.

What do you call soap all over the bathroom floor?
  Bubble trouble.

What do you call a fake horse?
  A phony pony.

What do you call a bird that loves sweet rolls?
  A muffin puffin.

What do you call a tired tent?
A sleepy tepee.

What do you call a pig in an earthquake?
Shaken bacon.

What do you call a werewolf professor?
A creature teacher.

What do you call a nap on a ship?
A cruise snooze.

Wacky Songs, Movies, and TV Shows

Weird Weather Reports

Clear Skies Forecast for Tonight by Esau Starrs

Tornado Touches Down! by Rufus Blownoff

Desert Storm Approaches by Dustin Mynose

Wacky Love Songs

"Kiss Me, Baby" by Puck R. Upp

"Walking in the Moonlight" by Holden Hanz

"I'm Nothing Without You" by M. T. Ness

"The First Time We Met" by Ken I. Havadate

"You're Wearing My Ring" by N. Gaged

"I'll Never Stop Loving You" by Percy Vere

"Don't Come Back Again" by Doris Shutt

"You're My Everything" by Trudy Light

"Why Did You Leave Me?" by Noe Clew

Wacky Video Games

Dragonslayer by Claude Chest

Superhero Blast by U. DaMann

Galaxy Wars by D. Stroid

NASCAR Speedsters by Red E. Setgo

Fairy Fantasy World by U. Nick Horn

Tarantula Attack! by Harry Leggs

Board Game Challenge by Bing O. Iwin

Wacky Movies

Jurassic Park starring T. Rex

The Wizard of Oz starring Ima Munchkin

Star Wars starring Ro Botts

Beach Blanket Bingo starring Sandy Trunks

Jaws starring Tay Kabite

I Was a Teenage Werewolf starring Harry Boddy

Wacky TV Reality Shows

Life of Crime starring Robin Banks

Real-Life Lottery Winners starring Jack Potts

Six Feet Under starring Paul Bearer

Weekend Warriors starring Gladys Friday

Olympic Ski Jumping starring Eileen Dover Toofar

Exploring Haunted Houses starring Hugo First

Extreme Hair Makeover starring Dan Druff

Gut-Busting Rides starring Rollie Coaster

Wacky Music Videos

"Move Your Body!" sung by Sheik Aleg

"Dance the Night Away" sung by Howell I. Evert Doothis

"I'll Never Dance Again" sung by Ferdie Lasttime

"Achy Breaky Heart" sung by Ann Guish

"Shake It Up, Baby" sung by Rock N. Rolle

"Reach for the Stars" sung by Tip E. Toes

"I'm Your Baby" sung by Todd Lerr

Wacky Advertisements

Buy Wondermint Toothpaste! call Pearl E. Teeth

Chew Our Sugar-Free Brand call Bub L.Gumm

Eat Our Organic Veggies call Hedda Lettuce

All-You-Can-Eat Buffet call I. M. A. Piggee

Instant Cash! Free! call A. T. M. Mashine

Sale on Greenhouse Flowers call Mary Golds

Old Furniture Refinished call Ann Teak

Wacky Personals

I'll Fix Your Car Today! call Mick Annick

Merry Maid Service call Dustin Taybles

New Guy Hair Salon call Buzz Cutts

Wanted: Pet Monkeys call Jim Panzee

Wanted: Ride to the Beach call Sonny Day

Creepy Critters

What should you wear when you go to the beach with a monster?
Sunscream.

How do monsters call their moms from the beach?
With shellular phones.

What beach creatures do monsters turn into when they get mad?

Crabs.

What's the best way to get a unicorn's attention?

Honk its horn.

Where do ogres work during the day?

At trollbooths.

Why was the troll so good in art class?

He lived under a drawbridge.

What kind of bridge is too small for a troll to live under?
The bridge of your nose.

Why can only one fairy sleep under a toadstool?
Because there isn't mushroom under there.

What do slugs put on their toes?
Snail polish.

What do ghosts read during band practice?
Sheet music.

Where do baby ghosts sit when they eat dinner?
In BOOster seats.

Where do witches park their vehicles?
In broom closets.

What's a witch's favorite computer tool?
Spell check.

What does a witch do before she opens her e-mail?
Types in her passwart.

What should you do if people say you look like a werewolf?
Go comb your face.

Why are spiders so popular online?
Each one has a Web site.

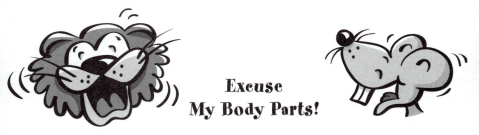

Excuse My Body Parts!

What did the skeleton say to the doctor?
  "I hope this doesn't cost me an arm and a leg!"

What did the body say to the skeleton?
  "I've got you under my skin."

What did the heart say to the liver?
  "Let's beat it out of here!"

What did the throat say to the bird-watcher?
  "I think I just saw a swallow!"

What did the eye say to the mouth?
  "One more word from you and you'll get fifty lashes!"

What talent does your cat have if she can read your mind?
  Extrasensory Purrception.

What kind of movies do frogs like?
  Sci-fly.

What does bubble gum become when it falls on a hot griddle?
  An unidentified frying object.

What do you call it when an extraterrestrial steals your jeans?
A clothes encounter.

Where should you take Dracula on his birthday?
To a stakehouse.

Why is it fun to play baseball with Dracula?
He has lots of bats.

Why is it fun to play baseball with Frankenstein?
He always keeps an eye on the ball.

Why aren't frogs allowed at baseball games?
They eat all the fly balls.

What do scientists use to get eels out of the ocean?
An eelbarrow.

What do slugs pack when they go on a trip?
Sluggage.

Where do city earthworms live?
In garden apartments.

What do centipedes eat for breakfast?
Scrambled legs.

Why did Little Miss Muffet scream?
She found a spider on her Web site.

What kind of hairdos do bees wear?
Buzz cuts.

Why do fleas never get cold?
They're always in fur coats.

Critter Chills

What should you send a sick elephant?
A get-wellephant card.

What should you send a sick ghost?
A BOOquet of flowers.

Where should you send a sick flea?
To a Lab.

Where should you send a sick mudfish?
To the detergency room.

Where can you find a sick rabbit?
On a hopperating table.

When should you eat fireflies?
When you want a light snack.

What should you say to a grumpy firefly?
"Lighten up!"

What do slugs put on their toes?
Snail polish.

What do mice like to eat at barbecues?
Grilled cheese.

What do mice wear when they shoot hoops?
Basketball squeakers.

Why do snakes ask for spoons?
Their tongues are already forked.

What do scorpions put on their hot dogs?
Scorpionions.

What Am I?

I'm full of keys but can't unlock a door. What am I?
  A piano.

I'm full of ink but can't write a word. What am I?
  A newspaper.

I have a deck but can't play cards. What am I?
  A ship.

I weigh hundreds of pounds but you can lift me with ease. What am I?
A scale.

I'm as light as a feather but hard to hold. What am I?
Your breath.

I work only when I'm fired. What am I?
A rocket.

I'm full of holes but can hold water. What am I?
A sponge.

I have a horn but can't honk. What am I?
A rhinoceros.

I'm long and skinny and short and round. What am I?
Spaghetti and meatballs.

I have eight ribs but no body. What am I?
An umbrella.

Is Any Body Here?

I have many teeth but can't chew. What am I?
A comb.

I have one eye but can't see. What am I?
A needle.

I have three feet but can't walk. What am I?
A yardstick.

I have hands but can't clap. What am I?
A clock.

I have ears but can't hear. What am I?
A cornstalk.

I make no sound until you say my name. What am I?
Silence.

I run around your yard but never move. What am I?
   A fence.

I run right up to your door but never come inside. What am I?
   A sidewalk.

I start with E and end with E, and have one letter inside. What am I?
   An envelope.

I have two banks but no money. What am I?
A river.

I have a bed but no sheets or pillows. What am I?
A flower garden.

I'm full of air but can't breathe. What am I?
A balloon.

I have two covers but no bed. What am I?
A book.

I have a ring but am not married. What am I?
A telephone.

I talk and sing but have no voice. What am I?
A radio.

I wave constantly but no one ever waves back.
What am I?
A flag.

I serve but never eat. What am I?
A tennis racket.

I have many stories but no windows. What am I?
A bookcase.

I run all day long but never leave your house.
What am I?
A refrigerator.

Bet You Can't Guess Me!

I'm clean when I'm black and white when I'm dirty. What am I?
A chalkboard.

My face turns red when I see you coming. What am I?
A stop light.

I get wetter the more I dry. What am I?
A towel.

I have good taste but never wear clothes. What am I?
A tongue.

I disappear when you stand up. What am I?
Your lap.

I disappear when you walk away. What am I?
Your reflection.

I have a trunk but use no gas. What am I?
An elephant.

I have lots of letters but no stamps. What am I?
A computer keyboard.

I'm full of people but no one's inside. What am I?
A television.

I wear a cap but have no head. What am I?
A mushroom.

I have a cone but no ice cream. What am I?
A volcano.

I hold your hand but we're not dating. What am I?
A glove.

Tongue Twisters

Bedspreads spread better on red beds.
Clean cashews crunch quite crisply.
Seashells sell swiftly sold seaside.

Sweet Treats

Swishy sushi chefs stir sticky shark strips.
Gooey guacamole grows great green globs.
Slurp sweet sloppy soup.
Buttered bran bread beats burned baked bagels.
Freshly fried fat flying fish from France.
A box of mixed biscuits makes the biscuits' box mixed.
Crisp cracker crusts crackle and crunch.

Critter Chitters

Wayne watches walruses wade in water.
Six sleek swans swam south swiftly.
Baboons buy bamboo by the bunch.
Lions like licking lemon lollipops.
Sheep should sleep in sheds.
Lazy lizards lick thick lovely lips.
Chris kissed six fish.

Buggle Wuggles

Six slimy snails squirmed silently down
slippery slopes.
Wiggly worms wriggle right away.
Blue bugs bleed blue-black blood.
Can clams cram into clean clam cans?
Selfish shellfish shall seek shelter.

Tongue Tiddles

Squish-squish, squids squirted swiftly.
Tick-tock, tick-tock, two chapel clocks
chimed clearly.
Caw-caw, cried crazy clawed crows.
Quack-quack quietly or quit quacking.
Bye-bye, bluebird, brown birds bawled.

Thongue Thwisters

Silly Seth sells thick socks and thin sweatshirts.

I wish to wash my wristwatch.

Six thick thistle sticks.

Blow beautiful blue balloons.

Rolling red wagons ride on real rear wheels.

Green glass globes glow gleaming.

Slim Tim shaves and shears six Swiss
sideburns.

Sports Shorts

Trey threw three free throws.

Surely the sun shall shine soon on soccer shirts.

Jessie jumped and jabbered joyfully.

Eve believes thieves seize skis with ease.

Keith kicks six sticks.

Ray's real rear wheel rode way rough.

Sixty sailors sail seven swift ships.

I'm Out of Here!

How fast do happy bikers ride?
Ten smiles per hour.

What's the best thing to take on a hot bike trip?
A thirst-aid kit.

Where do grizzlies put their bike bells?
On the handlebears.

What does a tornado do with a new car?
Takes it out for a spin.

What does a teacher do with a new car?
Gives it a test drive.

What vegetable can you use to polish your car?
Wax beans.

How does a kangaroo start a dead battery?
With jumper cables.

What's the best fuel to put in your lawn mower?
Grassoline.

Why don't mummies take vacations?
They're afraid they'll relax and unwind.

Why did it take so long for the bride to walk down the aisle?
She had a train on her dress.

Why are beavers like trains?
All day long they chew, chew, chew.

How can you get your dog to board a locomotive?
Train it.

In which part of a train do ghosts ride?
The caBOOse.

Car Tunes

What did the jack say to
the car?
  *"Can I give you
  a lift?"*

What did the driver say to the rabbit?
  "Hop in!"

What did one tire say to the other tire?
  "Want to go around together?"

What did one directional signal say to the
other?
  "Hey, it's my turn!"

What did the bumper say to the fender?
  "I had a smashing time today."

What did the wiper say to the
windshield?
  "What's bugging you today?"

What did the car say to the bridge?
  "You make me cross!"

How is a firefly like a car?
  They both have taillights.

When is it dangerous to be in the ocean up to your ankles?
When you're upside down.

Who should you call if you don't feel like paddling your own canoe?
A rowbot.

What do kings ride around their castles?
Moatercycles.

Let's Eat Out!

What did the cream say to the mixer?
  "I'm beat!"

What did the spaghetti say to the cheese at midnight?
  "It's pasta my bedtime."

What did the hot dog say to the barbecue?
  "I'd like you to meat my grillfriend."

What did the turkey say to the dressing?
  "I'm stuffed!"

What did the broth say to the vegetables?
  "You're souper!"

What did the beef say to the oven?
  "Turn down the heat . . . I'm roasting!"

What are penguins' favorite fast food?
  Icebergers.

Bye-Bye!

How do you say good-bye to a crocodile?
"Later, alligator!"

How do you say good-bye to a yardstick?
"So long!"

How do you say good-bye to a bad cold?
"Catch you later!"

How do you say good-bye to a trumpet?
"Tootle-oo!"

How do you say good-bye at the mall?
"Buy-buy!"

How do you say good-bye to an ocean?
Don't say anything . . . just wave.

Who would you call to perform in a sea circus?
The clown fish.

What's a cow's favorite amusement park ride?
The dairy-go-round.

What do gorillas love at a playground?
The monkey bars.

What's the first thing ghosts do on an airplane?
Buckle their sheet belts.

Why do cows take nonstop flights?
They love the long moooovies.

What's the best way to get from an airport to the beach?
By taxicrab.

Wacky Books, Magazines, and News Headlines

Wacky Joke Books

Stand-Up Comedians by Ima Clowne

Super Sidesplitting Jokes by Buster Gutt

Insults and Bloopers by Jess Joe King

Wacky Newspaper Headlines

DRACULA STRIKES AGAIN! by E. Drew Blood

DOGS ESCAPE THE POUND by Gay Topen

TOWN BUDGET VETOED! by Major Setback

SILVER MINE EXPLODES! by Dinah Mite

LOCAL LIBRARY 100 YEARS OLD by Annie Versary

PRISON LOCKED DOWN by Dora Steele

RESIDENT STREAKS THROUGH PARK by Running Bear

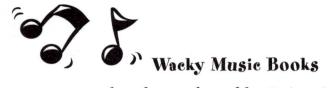

Wacky Music Books

How to Play the Keyboard by P. Ann Noe

Band Lessons by Claire A. Nett

Learn to Sing Beautifully by Sara Nade

Sopranos and Tenors by Al Toe

Tuning Your Guitar by G. M. I. Flatt

Orchestra Lessons by Phil Harmonick

Today's Top Hits by C. D. Player

Overcoming Stage Fright by Terry Fide

Wacky Ads

New Dentist Office Opens call Phil McAvity

 **Sale! Fresh Vegetables** call Brock O'Lee and Tom Atoe

Eat at Joe's Restaurant call Dee Lishus

New, Improved Bug Repellant call Amos Quito

Pack-Em-Up Moving Service call M. T. Rooms

Saturday Night Prayer Service call Neil Downe

Wacky Travel Books

Chased by a Lion by Claude Bottom

Swimming with Penguins by I. C. Waters

How I Survived in the Desert by Rhoda Camel

Europe on Foot by Misty Train

Scuba Diving for Beginners by Coral Reefe

Skydiving Made Simple by Perry Shute

How I Hid from Cannibals by Doug A. Hole

Walking Across Australia by Noe Otto Mobeel

Wacky Magazine Articles

"Why Doesn't Anyone Love Me?" by I. Malone

"How to Prepare a Picnic Lunch" by Phil D. Basket

"Raising Frogs in Your Backyard" by Lily Pond

"My Chocolate Obsession" by May I. Havesum

"The Dangers of Plastic Surgery" by Carver Upp

"Dandelions No More!" by Moe M. Downe

"Embarrassing Moments" by Sawyer Undees

"Fifteen Simple Makeup Tricks" by I. Shaddoe

"Quick Dinner Recipes" by Cassie Roll

"The Best Italian Soup" by Minnie Stroney

"Grow Basil and Oregano" by Herb Garrden

Silly School

In what school do you greet people?
  "Hi!" school.

What kind of adult has tiny pupils?
  A kindergarten teacher.

Why should you carry books on your head?
  So the teacher can read your mind.

Why did the teacher write on the window?
He wanted the lessons to be really clear.

How can you tell if math teachers dye their hair?
You can see their square roots.

What do music teachers tell their students?
To B-sharp.

What do students learn in night school?
To read in the dark.

When do students fail driver's ed?
When they're in a no-passing zone.

I Love School!

What should you tell your favorite geology teacher?
"This class rocks!"

What should you tell your favorite history teacher?
"I've been waiting for ages to take this course."

What should you tell your favorite math teacher?
"You're number one!"

What should you tell your favorite gym teacher?
"This class is a ball!"

What should you tell your favorite principal?
"You have a lot of class!"

How do baby fireflies learn math?
With flash cards.

Why was the moth afraid to give an oral book report?
It had butterflies in its stomach.

Computer Class

What do computers do in the cafeteria?
  Take a byte.

What equipment do aardvarks buy with their software?
  Aardware.

What should you do if your computer crashes?
  Take away its driver's license.

What's an astronaut's favorite computer key?
  The space bar.

What do you call a kitten that borrows your homework?
  A copycat.

Where did Sir Lancelot learn to slay dragons?
  In knight school.

Why are English teachers helpful?
  They always give the write answers.

Why was the biology student transferred?
  He was in dissection when he should have been in dat section.

Why do students attend summer school?
Summer smart, summer dumb.

What's the best way to get rid of a bad grade?
Erase it.

What's better than playing school?
Playing absent.

How do schoolbooks communicate?
With pagers.

What do hog students write with?
Pigpens.

Where do hogs keep their lunch money?
In piggy banks.

What's the best paper to write in a stream?
Your brook report.

Your Attention, Please!

What did the teacher say to the eyeball?
"Are you one of my pupils?"

What did the teacher say to the hot dog buns?
"Time for roll call!"

What did the teacher say to the golfer?
"Can you count to fore?"

What did the teacher say to the elf?
"Did you finish your gnomework?"

What did the teacher say to the octopus?
"Please raise your hand, hand, hand, hand, hand, hand, hand, hand."

How do kangaroos do their math homework?
With pocket calculators.

What should you do when a polar bear copies your homework?
Give it a cold stare.

What kind of stories do little horses read in kindergarten?
Ponytales.

What does dragon do when it misses school bus?
Dragon fly.

Where do religious-school students have recess?
On the prayground.

Why do principals always visit math classes?
They're the rulers of the school.

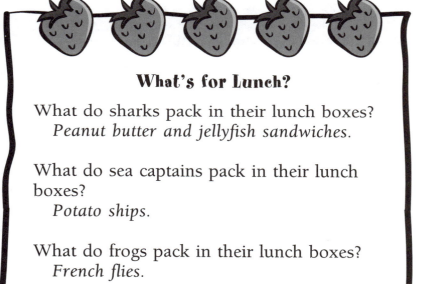

What's for Lunch?

What do sharks pack in their lunch boxes?
Peanut butter and jellyfish sandwiches.

What do sea captains pack in their lunch boxes?
Potato ships.

What do frogs pack in their lunch boxes?
French flies.

What do rabbits pack in their lunch boxes?
Carrot sticks.

What do cowboys pack in their lunch boxes?
Salad with ranch dressing.

What do scarecrows pack in their lunch boxes?
Strawberries.

Where do chickens find information for their term papers?
  In the hencyclopedia.

How do fish paint in art class?
  With watercolors.

What's the most important thing to write on a test?
  Your name.

Crazy Crosses

What do you get when a pig takes karate lessons?
  Pork chops.

What do you get when a gymnast flips over a dandelion?
  A tumbleweed.

What do you get when you put dirt in a race car?
  Quicksand.

What do you get when a shellfish mows your lawn?

Crab grass.

What do you get when a cow takes belly-dancing lessons?

A milk shake.

What do you get when a cat sits in your tree?

A pussy willow.

What do you get when you bungee jump with a sore throat?
A cough drop.

What do you get when your limas are covered with jam?
Jelly beans.

What do you get when you read a book on the beach?
Sandpaper.

What do you get when you lay your head on a bongo?
An eardrum.

What do you get when you put a purse in your bed?
A sleeping bag.

What do you get when a boulder falls on your submarine sandwich?
Rock and roll.

What do you get when you put a twig in your mouth?
Lipstick.

What do climbers get when they carry a stove up Everest?
A mountain range.

Creature Crosses

What do you call chickens with pockets?
Kangaroosters.

What do you call striped horses that swing on vines?
Chimpanzeebras.

What do you call animals that bury their horns in the ground?
Rhinocerostriches.

What do you call huge river animals that love snow?
Hippolarbears.

What do you call green garden reptiles?
Broccolizards.

Yummy Crosses!

What do you get when your pepperoni slides downhill?
Pizza rolls.

What do you get when a cow eats margarine?
Buttermilk.

What do you get when a steer eats a tadpole?
  A bullfrog.

What do you get when a frog sits at your kitchen counter?
  A toadstool.

What do you get when your dad eats an ice cube?
  Cold pop.

What do you get when you eat ice cream in a fir tree?
  Pinecones.

What do you get when glue sticks to your grandpa's dentures?
Toothpaste.

What do you get when you cross a praying mantis with a termite?
A bug that says grace before eating your house.

What do you get when you grill a brown cracker?
A grahamburger.

What do you get when your teacher becomes a vampire?
Blood tests.

What do you get when a bunny fixes your flat tire?

A jackrabbit.

What do you get when a critter eats a yellow-skinned fruit?

A bananimal.

What do you get when a movie actor takes your picture?

A shooting star.

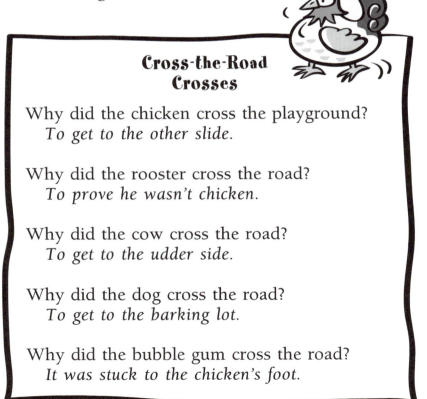

Cross-the-Road Crosses

Why did the chicken cross the playground?

To get to the other slide.

Why did the rooster cross the road?

To prove he wasn't chicken.

Why did the cow cross the road?

To get to the udder side.

Why did the dog cross the road?

To get to the barking lot.

Why did the bubble gum cross the road?

It was stuck to the chicken's foot.

What do you get when you lay your karate sash on a chair?
A seat belt.

What do you get when skeletons pray for birthday presents?
Wishbones.

What do you get when you put alphabet blocks in the freezer?
Ice cubes.

Goony Giggles

What award do you get for eating your veggies?
  The Nobel Peas Prize.

If you eat cinnamon rolls for breakfast and whole-wheat rolls for lunch, what do you eat for dinner?
  Casseroles.

What should you do if you have fat hair?
  Dye it.

What do rock climbers get their milk in?
Quartz.

What kind of flower is in your eye?
An iris.

What trees make good pets?
Dogwoods and pussy willows.

If gardeners plant flower bulbs, what do
electricians plant?
Lightbulbs.

Where does a volcano cook its dinner?
On a mountain range.

When should you put a diamond ring in your soup?
When the recipe calls for carrots.

What do umpires say when their cakes explode in the oven?
"Batter up!"

What's the first thing a karate instructor does on an airplane?
Fastens his black belt.

How does a minister pray when he has a cold?
On his sneeze.

What's the hardest part about learning to skateboard?
The pavement.

What's a snowboarder's least favorite season?
Fall.

Why are so many baseball players in jail?
They're always stealing bases.

Who do you call when beachboys won't go to sleep?
The Sandman.

Silly Smoochies

What did the house say to the bell?
"I adoor you."

What did the mitten say to the hand?
"I glove you very much."

What did the bee say to the rose?
"You're my honey."

What did the salt say to the sugar?
"How did you get so sweet?"

What did the lipstick say to the mascara?
"Let's kiss and makeup."

What did the candle say to the flashlight?
"Will you go out with me?"

What did the bubble gum say to the shoe?
"I'm stuck on you."

Why do carpenters have bad teeth?
They're always biting their nails.

Where's the best place to have a good cry?
Under a weeping willow.

How do you measure your lawn?
With a yardstick.

What do you call grass on the moon?
AstroTurf.

How do you find a cow in space?
Follow the Milky Way.

Why do distant stars pass out?
They're very faint.

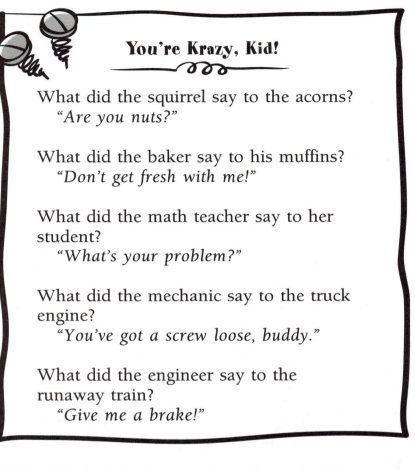

You're Krazy, Kid!

What did the squirrel say to the acorns?
"Are you nuts?"

What did the baker say to his muffins?
"Don't get fresh with me!"

What did the math teacher say to her student?
"What's your problem?"

What did the mechanic say to the truck engine?
"You've got a screw loose, buddy."

What did the engineer say to the runaway train?
"Give me a brake!"

What kind of drink does Santa bring bad boys and girls?
Coal-a.

What kind of vegetables could help you fly a kite?
String beans.

What should farmers do if crows steal their corn?
Call the crops.

Who leads the wedding party when two bakers marry?
The flour girl.

Why did the coffee taste like dirt?
It was just ground this morning.

What's the best snack to eat in a swamp?
Marshmallows.

What do zookeepers eat for snacks?
Animal crackers.

What do photographers eat for snacks?
"Cheese!" sticks.

What do killer whales eat for snacks?
Potato ships.

What do fathers eat for snacks?
Popcorn.

Why did the police raid the refrigerator?
The milk went bad and the apples turned rotten.

Where do crocodiles store their food?
In refrigergators.

What do you get when your lawn mower goes out of control?
Stained-grass windows.

What's the richest kind of air?
Billionaire.

What do sunglasses say when they marry?
"Eye do."

For Your Ears Only

Did you hear the joke about the flying saucer?
Never mind. It's way over your head.

Did you hear about the onion movie?
It's a real tearjerker.

Did you hear about the new jacket fastener?
It's a snap to open.

Did you hear about the volcano's birthday party?
It was a blast.

Did you hear about the telephone company's charity dinner?
It was a cellout.

Did you hear about the grass that left the soccer team?
It was cut.

Did you hear about the girl who wore a diaper hat?
She liked to change her mind.

Did you hear about the rodeo cowboy who became rich?
His horse was always giving him a buck or two.

Did you hear about the bread baker?
She got paid for loafing.

Did you hear about the invisible man?
He's totally out-of-sight.

Did you hear about the dog at the flea circus?
He stole the show.

Did you hear about the squirrel that found a 20-pound acorn?
He went nuts over it.

Aaa-choo!

Did you hear about the
sick elevator operator?
She's having her ups and downs.

Did you hear about the sick computer?
It caught a virus.

Did you hear about the programmer who
sneezed on his computer?
He had a code in his nose.

Did you hear about the sick zookeeper?
She's lion down right now.

Did you hear about the sick vampire?
He can't stop coffin.

Did you hear about the doctor with a
short temper?
He was always out of patients.

Did you hear about the sick frog?
It thought it was going to croak.

Did you hear about the patient who
swallowed a spoon?
He can barely stir.

Did you hear about the slow deck of cards?
It just shuffled along.

Did you hear about the hairstylist who used the wrong shampoo?
She could have dyed over it.

Did you hear about the angry exterminator?
He didn't like to be bugged when he was working.

Did you hear about the tame mosquitoes?
They'll eat right out of your hand.

Did you hear about the janitor robber?
He made a clean getaway.

Did you hear about the part-time chimney sweep?
The job soots him fine.

Did you hear about the woman who bought a
pair of snow tires?
They melted before she got home.

Did you hear about the boy who kept his guitar
in the refrigerator?
He liked to play cool music.

Chow Time!

Did you hear about the new pizza movie?
It's really cheesy.

Did you hear about the lost
pepperoni?
It's been going around in circles.

Did you hear about the smart chopsticks?
They're always using their noodles.

Did you hear about the hamburger that lost
the marathon?
It couldn't ketchup.

Did you hear about the boy
who stole hot dogs?
He was very frank about it.

Did you hear about the grapefruit that had a
baby?
It's just a little squirt.

Did you hear about the lonely banana?
It just wanted to be one of the bunch.

Did you hear about the macaroni
that fell asleep?
It was pasta their bedtime.

Catching
ZZZZZ

Did you hear about the girl who slept on her toaster?
She popped out of bed each morning.

Did you hear about the tired woodcutter?
He slept like a log.

Did you hear about the man who slept with a blanket over his head?
He's an undercover agent.

Did you hear about the sleepy reporter?
She worked for a snoozepaper.

Did you hear about the astronauts who couldn't eat dessert?
They'd just had a big launch.

Did you hear about the basketball player with a lasso?
He tied up the score.

Did you hear about the two walls that went on a date?
They met at the corner.

Did you hear about the two rubber bands that eloped?
It was a snap decision.

Did you hear about the judge who dressed like a skunk?
She always called for odor in the court.

Did you hear about the human cannonball?
He thinks he's a big shot.

Did you hear about the clerk who sold bagels?
She's the toast of the town.

Did you hear about the boy who yelled "Margarine!"?
I couldn't have said it butter myself.

Did you hear about the student named Rover?
He's the teacher's pet.

Did you hear about the cat that drank lemonade?
It was a real sourpuss.

Did you hear about the cat that ate a ball of yarn?
She had a litter of mittens.

Did you hear about the sock that escaped from the dryer?
It made a clean getaway.

Did you hear about the shark that dated a tuna?
They went out for a bite.

Did you hear about the jealous broccoli?
It was green with envy.

Did you hear about the stockings that missed the bus?
They had to run.

Did you hear about the golfer who left his sock on the fairway?
He got a hole in one.

Did you hear about the eagle's nest on the cliff?
It's a soar point.

Did you hear about the omelet joke book?
It's full of good yolks.

Did you hear about the boy who sat on a porcupine?
He got right to the point.

Index